Worton & Marston

A Community Remembers World War Two

Published by New Generation Publishing in 2022

First Edition

ISBN 978-1-80369-222-7

www.newgeneration-publishing.com

New Generation Publishing

Credits

The contents of this book are a written and photographic record of the event.

The individual family histories were compiled by relatives or individuals who donated them for public display and study at the event and as a permanent record (this book). They appear in this book in no specific order or level of importance. All information was provided by individuals for the public to view at the event and in any permanent record made of the event. All the individuals who provided information or family records are responsible for the content and accuracy of that information. It was provided freely for the public to view and record. All artefacts, such as medals, documents, helmets, uniforms were photographed then returned to the owners at the end of the event. All photographs were taken at the public event in the full knowledge of those participating in the event.

We would like to thank the following people and organisations for their support and contributions to the event.

People who contributed family records or artefacts for the event:

Keith Bridges, Pat Barton, Phyliss Martin, Marlene & Roger Wilshire, Robert Dodd, Peter Weston-Boddon, Robin & Judy Shercliff, Andrei Kostyszyn, Jill Duckworth, Chris Nixon, Veronica Franklin, Jackie Butler, Andrew Bonfield, Sally & Giles Collins, Paul Sperring, Dave Loveys, Philip Ferandez, Bryn Evans, Graham Davison, Di Tatlock, Keith Wright, Lorna Phillips, David and Christine Johnson, Jean Lane. Event photographs: Mark Fisher and David Johnson.

The Wessex Tommies (Steve Ottaway, Mark Hook and Andrie Kostyszyn). All those helpers over the weekend, supplying refreshments and acting as safety stewards. Also Paul Ganuszko for the slide presentation.

Worton Parish Council for insuring the event and also supporting the publication of this book with a grant from the Solar Farm Fund.

Worton and Marston Village Hall committee for the free use of the hall.

Proceeds from the sales of this publication will be split between **Worton and Marston Village Hall and Christ Church Worton.**

Chris and David Johnson

It has been 75 years since the end of WW2. This is how Worton and Marston community remembered.

What a year 2020 has been. This event all organised and ready for May of that year, was halted by the global pandemic. All events were cancelled.

However we could not let such a major event go by without recognition. So a covid-secure drive through the villages was organised and took place on VE Day 8 May 2020. Two cars were decorated with flags and wartime music was played. The cars drove through Worton and Marston and people were encouraged to hang out flags and stand in their front gardens and join in the festivities by singing. There was so much response after being in lockdown in their homes. The glorious weather brought people out, they smiled and cheered from their gardens.

However there was so much personal family wartime histories and documents submitted by people for the originally planned 2020 event, and great disappointment it had to be cancelled. It was decided that the event should take place in 2021, once covid 19 restrictions had been lifted.

The event took place on 21/22 August 2021 with a fantastic response. Many family histories and artefacts. The local WW2 enthusiasts brought vehicles and uniforms and many items of wartime equipment. Many people visited over the weekend. It was wonderful to see many of the older villagers meeting up for the first time after so long having to shield at home. So many smiles and stories being told. Once again a fantastic time was had by all visitors. **All monies raised at the event went to SSAFFA and Scotties Little Heroes.**

The village drive-through 8 May 2020

The event 21 – 22 August 2021

Family records of those living locally during the war

Poulshot and Worton Home Guard

Front Row left to right

1? 2? 3? 4 Arthur Early 5 Jimmy Ellis 6 Jack Bridewell 7 Ted Bridewell 8 John Cox 9? 10? 11 Dick Cox

2nd Row

1? 2? 3Bert Collect 4? 5? 6? 7? 8? 9 Tom Crockham 10 Birt Brown 11? 12 Jack Moyes

3rd Row

1Freddy Strange 2 Ern Axford 3 Percy Scratchley 4? 5? 6? 7 Eric White 8 Philip Oram 9 10 11 12 Tom Brown

Top Row 1 Eddie Fielding 2 Billy Jones 3? 4? 5? 6? 7? 8? 9? 10? 11? 12? 13?

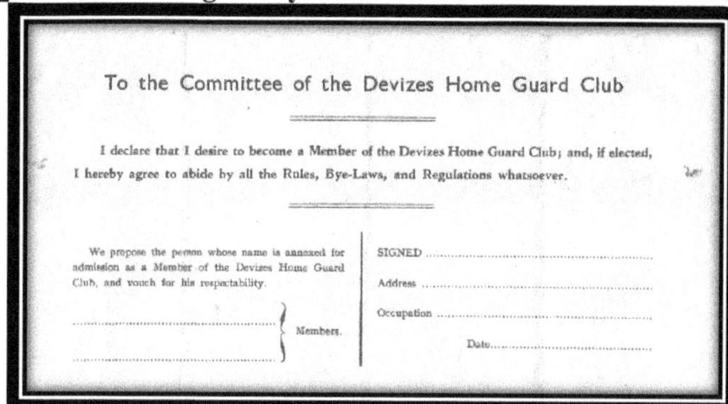

To the Committee of the Devizes Home Guard Club

I declare that I desire to become a Member of the Devizes Home Guard Club; and, if elected, I hereby agree to abide by all the Rules, Bye-Laws, and Regulations whatsoever.

We propose the person whose name is annexed for admission as a Member of the Devizes Home Guard Club, and vouch for his respectability.

.... } Members.
....

SIGNED ....

Address ....

Occupation ....

Date....................................

Bottom Row Seated

1. Bill Clack 2 Bert Butler 3 Jack Noyes 4 Harry Bowden 5 Percy Scratchley 6 Sam Ashley 7 Philip Fielding Alf Hale 8 Bert Collett 9 Tom Crocum 10 Tommy Dean 11 Alf Hale 12 Tom Brown

2nd Row

1. Billy Jones 2 Arther Axford 3 John Cox 4 Reg Philips 5 Eric White 6 Birt Brown 7? 8 Ern Axford 9 Freddie Strange 10 Bill Leake

3rd Row

1 Harold Pike 2 Bill Moxham 3 Ted Bridewell 4? 5 Mr Ellis 6 Dick Parrot 7 Len Turner 8 Arthur Bridewell 9 Bert Jeffries

4th Row

1? Feltham 2 Philip Oram 3 Dennis Stratley 4 Ted Gingel

Top Row

1 Mr Bowsher. 2 Fred Goodall. 3? 4 Ronald Goss

Photo courtesy of Jimmy Ellis Family

Serial No. 510.

A.F.W 4026.

Certificate of Proficiency

HOME GUARD

On arrival at the Training Establishment, Primary Training Centre or Recruit Training Centre, the holder must produce this Certificate at once for the officer commanding, together with Certificate A if gained in the Junior Training Corps or Army Cadet Force.

PART I. I hereby certify that (Rank) Cpl. (Name and initials) Cox J. of "F" ~~Battery~~ Company 4th. Wilts. ~~Regiment~~ Battalion HOME GUARD has qualified in the Proficiency Badge tests as laid down in the pamphlet "Qualifications for, and Conditions governing the Award of the Home Guard Proficiency Badges and Certificates" for the following subjects :—

	Subject	*Date*	*Initials*
1.	General knowledge (all candidates)	4·6·44	RCF
2.	Rifle	4 6 44	[illegible]
3.	36 M Grenade	4.6.44	RGB
*4.	(a) Other weapon Sten	11 6 44	[illegible]
	(b) ~~Signalling~~		
*5.	(a) Battlecraft, (b) ~~Coast Artillery~~, (c) ~~Heavy A.A. Bty. work~~, (d) ~~"Z" A.A. Battery work~~, (e) ~~Bomb Disposal~~, (f) ~~Watermanship~~, (g) M.T.	11 6 44	[illegible]
*6.	(a) Map Reading, (b) ~~Field works~~, (c) ~~First Aid~~	4 6 44	[illegible]

Date 4. 6 1944 Signature [illegible] Capt. R.A.
* President or Member of the Board.

Date 11 – 6 – 1944 Signature [illegible] Major
* President or Member of the Board.

Date ______ 194__ Signature ______
* President or Member of the Board.

Date ______ 194__ Signature ______
* President or Member of the Board.

Date ______ 194__ Signature ______
* President or Member of the Board.

PART II. I certify that (Rank) Cpl. (Name and initials) Cox J. of "F" ~~Battery~~ Company 4th. Wilts. ~~Regiment~~ Battalion HOME GUARD, having duly passed the Proficiency tests in the subjects detailed above in accordance with the pamphlet and is hereby authorized to wear the Proficiency Badge as laid down in Regulations for the Home Guard, Vol. I, 1942, para. 41d.

Date 16th June 1944 Signature [illegible] Lt. Col.
Commanding 4th. Wilts H.G. H.G.

PART III. If the holder joins H.M. Forces, his Company or equivalent Commander will record below any particulars which he considers useful in assessing the man's value on arrival at the T.E., P.T.C., R.T.C., e.g. service, rank, duties on which employed, power of leadership, etc.

Date ______ 194__ Signature ______
O.C.

* Delete where not applicable.

In the years when our Country
was in mortal danger

John Cox

who served 11 June 1940 - 31 December 1944
gave generously of his time and
powers to make himself ready
for her defence by force of arms
and with his life if need be.

George R.I.

THE HOME GUARD

Relative of Marlene Wilshire

Family of Roger Wilshire

Family of Peter Weston-Boddon

Peter Weston-Boddon. Born 21.11.1933 Kensington. London.

1. I went to Oxford Garden School, Kensington. London
   In 1939, my parents were advised to send their children to the country for safety. On Saturday September 2nd. 1939 All the children from my school were met with buses, at our school. They took us to Paddington station. All the children had labels pinned to their jackets with their names on them, and evacuee on the back. I was 5 years old.
2. I can remember arriving at Devizes station & having to wait for the carriage in front of mine to unload, as the platform was too short. We then moved forward & got off the train.
3. We all walked to the Corn exchange, we were split by the W.V.S. into sections. And sent to various villages. A lady took myself & two other boys in her car. She left me with
   Two elderly ladies for the night. The next day she collected me, and took me & the two other boys to Hurst Farm, in Great Cheveral, now called Worton.
4. The farm was run by Mr. & Mrs. Cox. They had two children of their own. Katherine, aged 8 & Graham aged 2.
5. Mr.Mrs. Cox took the two boys & Mrs. Cox said, where is this little boy going, we do not have anywhere yet said the lady, Well we will take him, she said.
6. The two boys were brothers, John & Burt Longhurst. We all shared the same double bed together, & had a candle for light. In the house there was
   No heating, no double glazing, no electricity, { they used paraffin lamps}, no gas, { they cooked on a coal & wood range} No water, they had a hand pump. & outside toilets.
7. The next day, we looked around the farm, there were 4 horses, Their names were, Darky, Jolly, and Blossom & Prince. About 200 chickens wandering everywhere. 80 to 100 cows & pigs.
8. Our school was the Library hall, the teachers were from our school in London. We had to walk to school each day which was About two miles. We took sandwiches for our dinner. And we went to Worton church on Sundays for Sunday school.

Before going to church we all shared a tin bath filled with two kettles of hot water for all five of us, starting with the youngest. One day leaving school, I went to the shop & bought what I thought was 2 chocolate squares costing 1p. each, they turned out to be exlax!!!!!

9. Sadly Graham passed away, in December 2016. Katherine is in a home in Market Lavington. I was at Hurst Farm for 3 & half years and return to help with the Hay making in my school holidays for several years. When we follow behind the horse drawn binder, { we did not have Combine harvesters then} We would catch the rabbits by hand, & give them to the villagers, for dinner.

10. In those days, Devizes market square was a livestock market, fall of cages of rabbits, chickens, duck, Geese. The Shambles was where all the calves were tied up. The back of the Shambles, now a car park, was the cattle market. I was lucky enough to get a ride in the horse pulled milk flout to the market.

11. It is interesting to note that we had Italian P.O.W's working on the farm, they would arrive daily by truck. Later we had German P.O.W's. The Italian's would collect the coloured string from the feed bags & plait & make slippers out of them. They also made me A ring out of a threepenny piece. As children we would go around the fields & hedgerows & collect wild rose hips, which The Government had asked to be collected to make rose hip syrup. It was our job to shut all the chickens up for the night, With small torches which when the batterys went flat, we would put them in the oven, as you could not buy batterys then. Two of the farm workers were Alf Hale, & his son, Cliff, The grandfather & father of June Mason

12. Having spent 3 & a half years at the farm, & coming back in my school holidays, it was a wonderful experience. Mrs. Cox must have been a saint, how she fed us all is a miracle.

The village is an example of friendly village life, and helpful people, I have never forgotten.

Additional Information.

I stayed for 3 & a half years. John Lonhurst & his brother Burt left after one year. Pam Bancroft & her sister Doris,{now in a care home} Worked in Harris's shop in Worton. Pam Bancroft lives 4 roads from me. Paul Neames died In 2011.

Our parents would come down from London 2 or 3 times per year & stayed from Friday until Sunday.

The Library Hall was our school. The boy's toilet was a tin shack outside. A big hole dug in the ground. At playtime we played on the

Cannon outside the hall which was a German trench cannon, we were told by the Clack family.

The Blacksmith, John Goss, would make cider in his press, from the apples, the farmers brought to him.

I have always kept in touch with the family all my life, & moved to Pottern in 1989, to Blounts Court.

In 2019 the BBC Country file programme contacted me regarding 1940's farming. I told them the story, & Adam Henson & the BBC visited the farm & said it was too dilapidated to use. We contacted The Countryside Trust who buy old farms & use them for educational purposes for today's children and for the future as this is the greatest event in living history and be should be kept for posterity, & for the sacrifices made could be remember especially for those villagers left to run the country side.

The farm is being taken care of by trusties.

Relatives of current villager's remembered

EARLY MEMORIES

By Jill Duckworth

I was born in 1938, one year before World War II began.

In approximately 1943 'The Americans' arrived. Some were stationed at Daylesford House – a large country house two miles from our village of Kingham in Oxfordshire. My father, a farmer would go several times a week to collect the unused food for the pigs. On one occasion I went with him in the pick-up where I had strict instructions to stay in the cab, Dad went off to see the person in charge when suddenly the cab was surrounded by black faces who were obviously cooks etc - never having seen a black person before I was a bit taken aback, but they were all smiling and offering me chewing gum so I didn't feel frightened.

At that time black G I's were not on the front line!

We had a British pilot, his Indian wife and their small son who was called Mickey living with us at that time. It was fun to have someone to play with, especially as Mickey had a toy car which I loved. Myself and Mickey were invited to a children's Christmas party in the officers mess at the RAF base in Chipping Norton, and I ate my first ever banana!

Luckily our pilot survived and apparently stayed in the RAF. He was a friend of Johnny Johnson who became a famous test pilot. There were several airfields around us and the RAF would drop strips of silver paper in the fields – including ours to help block radar information to the German planes. My friend Jenny (our foreman's daughter next door) and me would collect it and cut it up for confetti!

Another memory was 'The Home Guard' practising in the paddock. They didn't all have uniforms or guns in the beginning, but it was fun to watch them charging about while we were sitting on the bank. My two brothers were there too, and afterwards would play football with some of the younger members of the Home Guard – but of course, Jenny and I weren't allowed to play as 'girls don't play football!!

A young boy's memories of WW2 Bryn Evans

I lived with my parents and elder sister in a small village between Leicester and Melton Mowbray. My Dad failed his medical for the armed forces and so remained a baker as he did for the whole of his working life. During the war he worked every night with just Saturday night off. He cycled to work in all weathers covering 11 miles each way working an 8 hour shift in between. How times change! On nights off, he joined other men on ARP (Air Raid Patrol).

Life was not easy for families. As children, we were hardly aware of the difficulties our parents faced. We didn't really appreciate how difficult food rationing affected our mothers and fathers in trying to feed us. Having said that, poachers brought rabbit to our door late at night. Rabbit stew remains a real treat for me. My Grandad could keep a pig in his back garden. A huge family meant I didn't see much of the resulting meat. 'Hand me down' clothes were the 'norm'. Petrol rationing made travel difficult for public companies to offer a service and very few ordinary people had motorised vehicles anyway. I wish I could now tell my Mum and Dad how I appreciate their unselfish, loving sacrifices which we didn't realise at the time. In the 40/50s obesity was unknown as was public handouts.

My earliest memory is probably as a three or four, year old. My sister and I spent several nights under the dining room table as the

Luftwaffe bombed Leicester and Coventry. While we sheltered there, my mother sat in darkness by the fire with our next door, neighbours, a young woman and her elderly mother. The elderly male neighbour also worked nights. Riding his bike home early one morning he was knocked off and killed by some laughing louts in a lorry.

At some point, heavy bombing on London brought refugee children to our village as it did to communities across the country. I remember standing outside the village hall on a few occasions as women from the WVS (Women's Volunteer Service) handed over frightened children to (hopefully) well intentioned surrogate families. I felt sorry for these poor almost isolated children who suffered bullying from the local kids and some of the families charged with looking after them.

On the outskirts of the village there was a smallish Army Camp. One day, early in the war, we were in the backyard when a German plane was spotted flying around. My sister and I were quickly hustled inside and under the table. We later learned that the enemy plane had strafed a small cottage just a field away from the Army Camp.

It must be said that though my childhood memories are very clear, I did not keep a diary. Therefore, years stated will be taken from my knowledge of the progression of the war.

Eventually, the British soldiers moved out and the camp was used to house POWs. At first, we saw a large contingent of Italians. I guess this was 1942 as the British 8th Army made great gains in North Africa. The Italians were very innovative. Outside their Nissan hut type living quarters, they built mounds of earth and rocks which they then turned into miniature mountain villages with houses, churches and even working water mills.

Later, probably during 1944 as the Allies pushed the Germans forces back, the Italians were replaced by German prisoners who remained until well after the war ended. Eventually, the Germans were allowed out during certain times under strict curfew. Some were employed on local farms and I clearly remember a large gang digging out the banks and clearing debris from the village brook to prevent flooding. They were also innovative in that they would make small, wooden toys which they would give to us children. During the light, summer evenings the prisoners were allowed to walk through the village. I would often be sitting on the front step as would other children. For some reason, two of the POWs, Hans and Bern, became my very good friends. In addition to bringing me toys, they would bring rare treats such as roly poly pudding. How POWs could get food which we never saw still remains a mystery for me. During the very bad winter of 1947/48, they taught me how to slide and skate on the hard, frozen brook. Also, they showed me how to lie in the deep snow and make a bird impression. Later, as they neared release, they began to receive news from their homes. Poor Hans heard that his entire family had been wiped out. Sadly, he committed suicide in his prison hut. I still hold treasured memories of those two guys who probably didn't want to fight any more than our boys did.

I step back a little now to, I suppose, 1943 as the Allies began the build up towards the D Day invasion of mainland Europe. At Scraptoft, another village about 3 miles from mine, a huge force of US Paratroopers assembled. They conducted training and war games all over the local area including parachute drops during both day and night. Inevitably, there were many accidents, some with tragic endings. However, I recall one amusing case after a night time drop. An American paratrooper was found hanging from an apple tree. He had hung there all night without knowing he was only a few feet from the ground.

Suddenly one day, they all disappeared. D Day had taken place and the end was in sight. VE Day saw a street party in School Lane right outside my home. Memory says it was a huge feast, Reality says it probably wasn't that good due to continued food rationing but our mothers did their utmost and succeeded in making a small boy's memories very special. I wouldn't mind betting they blew a whole month's worth of Ration Coupons.

Throughout the latter years of war, we saw huge formations of bomber aircraft heading east towards targets in enemy held territory. Every night, weather permitting, the sky seemed full. Hundreds of slow, moving planes with their fighter escorts buzzing around them. I imagine these were the legendary 'thousand bomber raids'. Sometimes there were smaller formations circling our area. I was told these were squadrons waiting to be joined by squadrons from other airfields. Gradually, the numbers increased and then they were off.

Bryn Evans.

Family of Philip Fernandez

El Tanque

During a recent chat with a man I have known in business and as a friend for many years, I happened to mention the WW2 commemorations to be held in Worton weekending 21 August 2021.

He then told me of his father's remarkable journey as a young man from Spain which ended in Chippenham. His father's nick name was El Tanque (The Tank) so I guess he was a big man. During the Spanish Civil War (1936-1939) El Tanque was opposed to the dictator Franco. He was captured during a big battle in the north of Spain. (I suspect this might have been at Zaragoza). Along with many others, El Tanque was taken prisoner and deposited on the beach at Rosas. From here, together with huge numbers, he escaped across the Pyrenees into France. Although they were now safe, the French were not very helpful or welcoming. The refugees were left in fields with no shelter or help. So, they dug holes to provide themselves with some shelter. In order to survive, El Tanque and his friends volunteered to join the French Foreign Legion and were sent to Morocco.

When the Nazis invaded Norway, this section of the Legionnaires were deployed to assist the British in fighting the Germans. After service there, El Tanque and comrades were then put on a troop ship returning to Morocco. En route, the ship docked at Southampton. Here the troops took over the ship and refused to sail back to Morocco. Eventually, the British allowed them to disembark and housed them in a camp at Grittleton near Chippenham.

Spaniards from Grittleton and other Internment Camps across the country joined British troops on the D Day invasion of France. Those who returned were given British Citizenship. Many of these men eventually married local girls. Hence there are a lot of people around Chippenham descending from the adventurous Spanish fighters.

Bryn Evans with kind permission of Philip Fernandez

Family of Dave Loveys

My **Uncle**, mum's brother, joined the R.A.F. to train as a pilot. It was found that he suffered colour blindness and therefore wasn't able to fly. I don't know what happened after that, but assume he remained in the air force until the end of the conflict.

My **Father** was running his family farm at Doddiscomleigh, which is a village on the edge of Dartmoor about seven miles from Exeter. He was unable to join up due to 'Flat Feet' apparently, but did serve in the local Home Guard. They were guarding the water reservoirs that supply Torquay and I assume Exeter. I believe there was a worry that the Germans may try to contaminate the water supply. All this was before my Mother and Father even knew each other.

My **Mother**, who was a teacher, was teaching at a school in London when war broke out. Her family all lived in Wolverhampton, where she was born. I do know she had a History degree and that she gained it at Birmingham University. However how it happened I don't know, but she spent the war years at a school in Brayford, near Barnstable, North Devon. I believe she was evacuated from London with some of her pupils from school, but am not sure how it happened. Whatever, I am certain she spent time there. I can remember her telling both my brother and I that after the war she liked being in Devon so much that she applied for and got a teaching job at Doddiscomlegh. There she met my Father, and they married, I have never known the date, and in 1948 moved to 8 Mill Lane, Alfington, Ottery st Mary, where I was born in June of that year, and my brother nearly two years later. Some of my earliest memories are of long journeys to spend Christmas at Wolverhampton with my Grandparents, and fairly regular visits to Molland Farm, which is near Brayford, and is where my mother lodged during her time at Brayford. The Farmer and his wife had no children of their own and Roger and I were always made especially welcome there. Everyone concerned died long ago, but by chance, about twelve years ago I was delivering to a farm close to Molland Farm, and as the Farmer shared the same surname I asked him if he knew the owner of Molland Farm at that time. I was very surprised to find out that he was the owner's nephew, and that his father was still alive. Although well into his nineties the old man remembered my mother living at Molland farm during the war. He particularly remembered her helping on the farm at busy times after she got back from school. Had it not been for the war, I wouldn't be here!

Family of Graham Davison

Wilfred Davison Capt.

13th Battalion Parachute Regiment

Wilfred (Wilf) Davison was called up on 29th August 1939 at the age of 19 into the 4th Battalion Dorsetshire Regiment. He spent his first few weeks in the army in Portland where he was soon promoted to Corporal.

In January 1940 he was chosen to join a small party sent to join the 2nd Battalion Dorsets in France on a reconnaissance mission. It was here that he killed his first German and saw one of his company fall.

Shortly after, he returned to England and re-joined the 4th Dorsets and received his promotion to Sergeant. When volunteers were requested for parachute training, Wilf signed up immediately. He was sent to Chesterfield for extensive training before returning to Bulford Camp to join the newly formed 4th Battalion Parachute Regiment in 1942.

As part of this Battalion, Wilf was sent to North Africa in late 1942 where he took part in Operation Torch in Algeria and later with American forces in Tunisia.

After the success of the North African campaign, Wilf along with the Battalion parachuted into Sicily in July 1943 as part of the Allied Invasion, codenamed Operation Husky. Wilf's time in Sicily was short-lived as he was selected for officer training and was sent back to Algiers and from there back to England to complete his training.

After his training, he was posted to the 13th (Lancashire) Parachute Battalion in Larkhill where he took up command of No. 11 Platoon as their Lieutenant.

Wilf next saw action when he was sent to Belgium on 24th December 1944 (his wedding anniversary) where he took part in the Battle of the Bulge. He led one of two platoons into Bure to recapture the village. Eventually they succeeded but he was injured and taken to Louvain where a piece of shrapnel was removed from his back.

For his action in Bure and in recognition of his services towards Belgium he was awarded the Croix de Guerre avec Palme and the Order of Leopold avec Palme.

Following his recovery, Wilf next saw active service in March 1945 when the Battalion was engaged in the last airborne operation of the war, the River Rhine crossing. By then Wilf had been promoted to Captain. It was during this time in Germany that he took part in operations to clear a concentration camp at Belsen. This was an experience he would never forget and about which he never spoke in detail.

Following the VE Day celebrations, Wilf, along with the Battalion, was sent to India to conduct operations against the Japanese empire. However, the war ended before they could begin. As a result he then went to British Malaya, Singapore and Java to help disarm the Japanese occupiers and restore law and order before finally returning home in 1946.

Following the war, Wilf lived a long and happy life with his wife Phyllis and their 6 children; Keith, Dennis, Graham, Liz, Sheila and Helen. He passed away on 6th March 2016 aged 95 and is buried in Wootton Rivers with Phyllis.

1939
22
21-3-42
BOMBAY

Family of Robin Shercliff

Frank Shercliff in World War 2

After his Great War service in Gallipoli and the Somme Frank Shercliff returned briefly to Australia before emigrating to become a Chief Mining Engineer in Malaya to escape the Spanish Flu then raging in Melbourne. He was 52 when, as the Chief Engineer of the Tronoh Tin Mining Company, and with war with Japan looming, he joined the Local Defence Corps in Perak to watch the bush tracks crossing the frontier into Thailand.

When Japan invaded Malaya just hours before their attack on Pearl Harbour the Local Defence Force was united with the 1st Battalion Federated Malay States Volunteer Forces (Perak) to be used to reinforce the small, hard-pressed remnants of the 11th Indian Division. The generals decided there was to be no defence north of Ipoh which exposed Frank's mines at Tronoh – then the most productive in the world.

Ground forces became more and more hard pressed by Japanese military superiority and a general withdrawal behind the Perak River was ordered, at which Frank lost all his possessions. Using outflanking manoeuvres from the sea, the Japanese overcame the British forces and caused them to withdraw progressively to the south, at which point the Perak L.D.C. became a meaningless identity and Frank was ordered out to make his way south to join the Selangor Local Defence Corps. With them he withdrew from Kelantan when this battle was lost and fell back to Kuala Lumpur, which in turn was left when it fell to the Japanese after a successful outflanking amphibious landing at Port Swettenham. It was at this stage that the Federated States Volunteer Force was lost as a formed body because those Asiatic members who wished to stay with their families were not compelled to remain with their units. The great majority chose to hand in their arms and return home.

The Japanese pressed into Jahore State using bicycles and small craft and there was a further large-scale withdrawal from the area by

British, Australian and Indian forces. Nevertheless Frank, a WW1 sapper and mining engineer put his shoulder to this massive wheel during the relentless enemy onslaught.

Our forces withdrew to a new defensive line between Mersing and Batu Pahat but this didn't last long against Japanese pressure, and further retreats began almost immediately. Then a large enemy amphibious force landed at Endau and crossed the River Mersing so, with the expectation of losing the whole of our forces on the mainland, General Percival ordered a retreat across the Johore Straits to Singapore Island. A seventy-foot gap was blown in the Causeway and the battle of Singapore began.

Singapore

Frank made his own way to Singapore to join the Singapore Security Unit, with whom he remained until the capitulation. Large Japanese reinforcements mounted severe amphibious attacks through the mangrove swamps into Singapore itself and after massive supporting bombardments the enemy with their tanks mounted a ferocious final assault. With food, water, fuel and ammunition all practically exhausted and no strength left even to resist, and with a looming Japanese thrust into the town with all the atrocities that would bring forth, the decision was made to capitulate. The army of Malaya passed into captivity.

Changi Gaol

British and Australian troops were marched on a 14 hour journey to Changi Camp where 2,300 civilians were interned in Changi gaol. Changi prison, designed to take 800 prisoners, became the home of 3000 men and 400 women and children who for two years endured the nightmares and brutality within the prison's stone walls. The prison had cold, foul smelling cells, each cell crawling with bugs and each approximately 6ft x 8ft with a concrete block in the centre serving as a bed for one prisoner. Two more prisoners slept on the floor on either side. One small window approximately one foot square gave a little light and much needed fresh air, while a hole in the floor in one corner served as a toilet.

By early September 1942 the prisoners taken to Changi seven months earlier, numbered less than half. Many died of hunger and disease and many more had been taken to other destinations to be put to work as slaves. Frank himself contracted beri-beri and various other diseases associated with diet deficiency. The prisoners existed on a rice-based diet with virtually no protein or fats, and they received no Red Cross parcels for the whole of their internment. By 1944 they were in a bad way. Dysentery, malaria and pellagrous dermatitis were rife. Children's arms, legs and feet were covered with tropical ulcers. The sick could not be treated as there were no drugs and even the supply of bandages ran out. The plight of the men and boys was particularly acute because, despite just starvation rations, they were forced to carry out manual labour for the Japanese, including working on military projects.

By early September 1945, soon after Japan surrendered, over 17,000 men were congregated in the Changi Gaol compound, and medicines and medics were parachuted in to assist the suffering. After that the army mobilised a fleet of transports to return everyone home. Frank finally left Singapore in a troopship on the 24th September 1945. On his return to Australia his weight was down to 9 stone from his previous 15.

Church Service in Changi Chapel

The Original Changi Chapel

now in Australia

Changi Gaol during World War II

Inside Changi Gaol at Liberation

Starving Australian POWs

Changi Prison Singapore

Family of Judy Shercliff

Air Vice-Marshal Frank Dodd

AIR VICE-MARSHAL Frank Dodd, who has died aged 74, was an exceptionally skilled photographic reconnaissance pilot during the Second World War, in which he won the DSO, DFC, AFC and the Air Efficiency Award.

Dodd was also entrusted with such long-distance Mosquito courier tasks as delivering sensitive diplomatic mail to Moscow.

Having made his name reporting and photographing the battleship *Tirpitz* in her lair in a Norwegian fjord, Dodd made the first of 11 round trips in support of Winston Churchill's autumn 1944 talks with Stalin.

Dodd's flight in an unarmed sky-blue Mark XVI "Mossie" was eventful — though he did not run into the trouble he expected as he flew over the eastern front. His chief difficulty was to match the information on outdated RAF maps with the Russian terrain below.

Before setting out from Sumburgh in the Shetlands, his flight sergeant navigator, Eric Hill, had planned to read his way to Moscow like a weekend club flier following railway lines. But the lines were no longer there: the Russians had moved them.

As pilot and navigator attempted to distinguish one town from another, a formation of Russian fighters appeared on their tail, gave chase and opened fire with tracer, none of which found its mark. Dodd decided that the Russian pilots must either be bad shots or simply firing away to indicate comradely fervour.

Taking no chances, Dodd opened up to 330mph and left the fighters far behind. In Moscow the Russians could not do enough for the aircraft and its crew: vodka, caviare and seats at the Bolshoi were laid on, while the machine was serviced by ground crew with a suspiciously intimate knowledge of the Mosquito. Operation Frugal had hardly lived up to its codename.

Frank Leslie Dodd was born on March 5 1919 and educated at King Edward VI School, Stafford, and Reading University.

He joined the RAFVR as a pilot in 1938. Dodd's thoughtful, sometimes dour manner, coupled with remarkable flying ability, singled him out as an ideal flying instructor.

He took the Central Flying School course and from 1940 to 1944 contributed steadily to the flow of new pilots. In 1944 he was posted to No 544, a Mosquito reconnaissance squadron.

Dodd developed a great affection for the speedy little "Wooden Wonder", and would later quote Goering's wartime lament with relish: "I turn green with envy when I see the Mosquito. The British knock together a beautiful wooden aeroplane that every piano factory over there is building."

Maddened by the "Mossie's" elusive speed, Goering resorted to his surprise jet fighter, the Me 262 — which levelled the odds, as Dodd discovered. On Aug 18 1944 he was intercepted by a jet over Gebelstadt and dived 10,000ft to escape.

Then, near Munich on Sept 16, Dodd and Hill were attacked eight times by a pair of Me 262s. The jets attacked independently at almost 30,000ft in wide circles and sweeps, Dodd making tight turns as he descended. It was touch and go until he found cloud cover at 6,000ft.

Granted a permanent commission, in 1947 Dodd received command of No 45, a Beaufighter squadron in the Far East. The next year he returned home, serving on the Central Flying School staff at Flying Training Command, where he was appointed CFS Chief Instructor in 1953.

From 1955 he was heavily involved with the nuclear deterrent V-bomber force, beginning with command of No 230 Operational Conversion Unit at Waddington, where Vulcan crews were trained. In 1959 he was appointed group captain training at Bomber Command, and two years later station commander at the Coningsby Vulcan base.

Subsequently he returned to CFS as air officer commanding and commandant. In 1965 he was appointed director responsible for establishments at the Defence Ministry. Finally he was director-general of the Linesman Project management organisation from 1970 until he retired in 1974.

Dodd then became administrator of the MacRobert Trusts, endowed by Sir Alexander MacRobert, whose three sons were killed flying in the war and whose widow presented the RAF with three Hurricane fighters and a Stirling bomber ("MacRobert's Reply").

Dodd maintained the tradition of beneficence to the Service, arranging a £20,000 grant for playing fields at the RAF Benevolent Fund's Duke of Kent School and turning over the MacRobert seat in Aberdeenshire to the Fund, with £360,000 to build an extension.

Dodd was awarded the DSO and AFC in 1944, DFC in 1945, AE in 1945 and Bars to the AFC in 1955 and 1958. He was appointed CBE in 1968.

He married, in 1942, Joyce Banyard; they had a son and three daughters.

Family of Veronica Franklin

Maurice Jacques 1923 – 1955

This hat, belt and medals belonged to my uncle, my mother's brother. He was too young to enlist when the Second World War started and so he worked with his father in the ARP until he was 18.

He then joined the British Army and attained the rank of Major. I didn't ever know him as sadly he died in May 1955 at the age of 32 and I was born in October of that year but my mother often spoke fondly of him. He was ten years older than she and so she remembered as a child proudly walking out with him in his uniform when he came home on leave.

Veronica Franklin

Family of David Johnson

<u>Father</u> Alan Johnson (Below) at the outbreak of war he was in at school, Isle of Sheppey, Kent and witnessed some of the "small ships" flotilla which sailed across the English Channel to rescue the Allied forces from Dunkirk May 1940. He also witnessed first-hand the Battle of Britain dogfights over Kent during the summer of 1940. He was awarded a scholarship but gave it up to join the war effort at the Sheerness Navy dockyard. He carried out vital work in in Royal Navy dockyards at Sheerness, Chatham, Rosyth and Portsmouth. He survived the war and remained with the Royal Navy until his retirement in the 1980's. **He was awarded the Imperial Service Medal.**

<u>Mother</u> Ethel Johnson (Below) worked in a Lancashire cotton mill. She came from a family of coal miners, who had worked in the mines for generations. She was crowned Cotton Mill Queen on her 21st birthday in 1939, just a few weeks after war was declared. (See the photo below which was taken at the event). The cotton mill was subsequently converted into munitions factory, where she worked for the duration of the war. (Some of her friends were killed by accidental explosions). She described enduring German bombing raids on nearby Liverpool docks and Manchester factories. In particular the sustained raids during December 1940. Also the impact on the local

area of the arrival of American service men. She was discharged at end or war, however she joined the MoD and worked in the Navy Stores department until she got married.

Grandfather Ernest Johnson (Below) also carried out essential work in the Royal Navy Dockyards in Sheerness and Chatham in Kent. He came from a long line of Royal Navy dockyard workers. His brothers, father and grandfather had all been involved in the Royal Navy or ship building. He carried out this work during WWI and again during WW2. He was a boiler maker by trade and worked on the repair of naval vessels. He survived the war and remained with the Royal Navy until his retirement in the 1950's. **He was awarded the Imperial Service Medal.**

Uncle William Holland (Below) Brother of Ethel (Johnson), came from a family of coal miners, who had worked in the mines for

generations in Lancashire. He joined the 8th Army and fought in North Africa and Italy. He survived the war and returned home. Apart from family photos little detail is known about his wartime exploits.

Great Uncle James Holland (Below), Brother of Ethel (Johnson's) father, came from a family of coal miners, who had worked in the mines for generations in Lancashire. He served in different roles in both World Wars. He was an officer in WWI who survived and returned. In WW2 he was a member of the ARP and later became a Corporal in the Civil Defence. He passed away in 1944. Below WWI photo and WWII photo.

Uncle John Telford (Below) Brother-in-Law to Ethel (Johnson), came from Lancashire. He joined the 8th Army and fought in North Africa and Italy. He survived the war and returned home. Apart from family photos little is known about his wartime exploits.

Uncle William Osborne

Fought in North Africa and the Far East. Apart from family photos little is known about his wartime exploits. After the war he settled in Australia, where he mysteriously vanished. Below are photos of him and colleagues during the war and farming in Australia after the war.

Relatives of Chris Johnson: The Hill's

Many of my mother's family fought in WW1 and the children of these joined the forces in WW2, as soon as they were old enough.

My mother (Ivy Hill) came from a family of 6 children and they lived in Poplar in London's East End along East India Dock Road.

My Uncle George born 1924 was her oldest brother lied about his age (as many young boys did at that time) and joined the 8th Army when he was only 16 years old. He was in the force that attacked Monte Cassino where he was buried alive. Fortunately for him he was rescued but this experience affected him for the rest of his life. He continued to fight and post war was married and lived into old age.

Her sister Elsie (born 1931) joined the Wrens when she was old enough.

My mother (Ivy born 1926) and her younger brother James (born 1929) were evacuated to rural Wales. This they disliked so much that they both ran away and got back home to the East End. My mum was always resilient and was recruited to be a child messenger. This was a very dangerous occupation and many children died relaying these messages. When mum was old enough she joined the Wrens and consequently the Land Army where she was posted to the Isle of Wight and she met her lifelong friend Val.

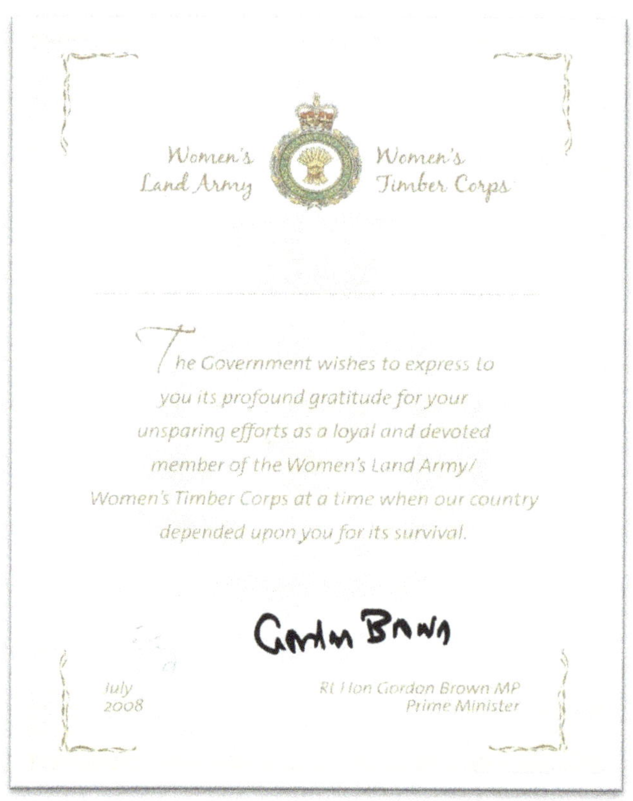
Women's Land Army

Women's Timber Corps

The Government wishes to express to you its profound gratitude for your unsparing efforts as a loyal and devoted member of the Women's Land Army/ Women's Timber Corps at a time when our country depended upon you for its survival.

Gordon Brown

July 2008

Rt Hon Gordon Brown MP
Prime Minister

From here Mum witnessed the D-Day embarkation for the invasion of France. That must have nerve racking and very emotional as I'm sure the realisation of what it meant was probably not fully understood at that particular time until news reports trickled home.

James joined the Merchant Navy towards the end of the war as a chef following in the family trade.

Their family home in the East End of London was bombed to the ground. The family bakery in Portsea Hampshire which has previously been sold was also bombed to the ground. (Mum died in 2013).

Her younger sister Joan (born 1933) was evacuated to Devon and saw the war out there. Later in life she joined the Queen Alexander Nurses.

Relatives of Chris Johnson: Charles Henry Spokes born 1902

My father Charles was a member of the home guard during the war and served along the Red Line which defended the River Thames, our last line of defence. He was assigned to the anti-aircraft guns which were based on the airfield where he worked. As he had been a member of the regular army between wars and was now in a reserved occupation.

He now worked for F.G Miles Aircraft Company, which was based at Woodley and Reading aerodrome. This aerodrome, from what I can gather was one of the most secret government locations during the war testing many prototype jet engines. His occupation was as an electrician wiring the new aircraft built there for the war.

(This engine development was suddenly halted and the design given to the Americans and became later known as Boeing 727).

After the war my father continued working for the government at the AWRE Aldermaston (Atomic Weapon Research Establishment). He worked here until he retired. He survived until just before his 90th. Charles is centre of photograph with the drums.

Reg Harvey born 1903

Another relative by marriage, Reg (born 1903) was in a reserved occupation working in the signal box on the railway. His signal box was located along the River Thames at Streatley, Berkshire.

One night he heard a terrible droning noise and looked to the sky where he saw many, many German bombers following the river. His words, "Some poor souls are going to get it tonight." Little did he know at the time Coventry was their target. Hours later he heard them return and news reports filtered through about Coventry being flattened. I cannot imagine how that must of felt. (He died age 99 years old).

Family of Robert Dodd

France summer 1944 Fred Dodd sitting in jeep with mates of Royal Corps of Signals

Five of Rob Dodd's six uncles who fought in WWII

Germany winter 1945 from left to right Simo, Bindon and Fred Dodd

Family of Paul Sperrings

Lorna Phillips

In the 1940's I was a member of the 4th Northwood (Middx) Girl Guides. Several of us spent Saturday mornings threading comfortable linings into tin hats of A R P personnel in the area.

In 1944 I travelled each day from Northwood Hills to Kilburn Polytechnic where I was doing a secretarial course. One evening I had just set off for home from Kilburn station when a V2 rocket landed quite near to the station.

<u>SO THAT WAS A LUCKY DAY!</u>

My brother Victor was born on V E Day.

Dennis Phillips

Family of Andrew Bonfield

Family of Keith Bridges. Family of Pat Barton.

Family of Jean Lane

Family of Andrei Kostyszyn

MINISTRY OF DEFENCE
APC DISCLOSURES 5 (POLISH)
Building 1 (Ops), RAF Northolt
West End Road
Ruislip, Middlesex HA4 6NG
Telephone: 020 8833 8600 Fax: 020 8833 8666
E-mail: NOR-PolishDiscOfficeAsst@mod.uk

Our Ref: 3/18810/APC/POL/K

Date: 1 April 2015

Dear Madam

Thank you for your recent enquiry. I am pleased to confirm the following particulars of the military service of:

30018810 – PRIVATE WŁADYSŁAW KOSTYSZYN

Born on: 25 April 1921 (not 24 April 1924) **at** Krechówka, Stryj, Stanisławów, Poland

Parents: Bronisław and Antonina née Marek

Marital Status (while serving): Single

Nationality: Polish **Religion:** Roman Catholic

Civilian Occupation (prior to Army Service): Farmer

Service with the Polish Forces under British Command:

from 1 April 1942 **to** 20 January 1947

Service with the Polish Resettlement Corps: Enlisted on 21 January 1947
Commissioned

relegated to:
Class "W" Reserve on 5 July 1947
Unemployed List

finally discharged 14 January 1948
relinquished commission on
(honourably discharged)

Conduct: Good

Former Service and History:

Prior to 1939 lived at Krechówka, Balicze, Stryj, county of Stanisławów, Poland (now Ukraine), which after the 1939 September campaign in Poland was occupied by the former Soviet Union. Being of Polish nationality, he was deprted to the former USSR – exact date(s) and place(s) of his deportation/forced labour within the former USSR not recorded.

Released on the basis of the Sikorski-Maisky (Polish-Soviet) agreement of 30 July 1941, together with the Polish Army units, crossed the Soviet-Iranian border and was evacuated to Iran. Enlisted in the Polish Forces under British command in Iran with effect from 01.04.1942. Via Iraq was transferred to Palestine.

On the re-organisation of the Polish Army in the Middle East was posted to 5 Light Anti-Aircraft Artillery Regiment, 5 Kresowa Infantry Division, 2 Polish Corps, 8 British Army on 06.02.1943.

Served in the Middle East (Iran, Iraq, Palestine, Egypt) 1942-1944 and in Italy 1944-1946, when together with 2 Polish Corps was transferred to the United Kingdom – exact date of arrival in the United Kingdom not recorded.

Due to a gradual demobilisation of the Polish Forces under British command, enlisted in the Polish Resettlement Corps (PRC) and served in the United Kingdom until finally discharged on 14.01.1948 on absorption into industry.

Theatre of Operations:

Italy 15.02.1944 – 02.05.1945

15.02.44-23.04.44	Action on the Rivers Sangro and Rapido/Southern Apennines
23.04.44-31.05.44	Battle for Monte Cassino/Gustav-Hitler line of enemy defences
01.06.44-04.09.44	Battle for Ancona/Goths line of enemy defences
05.09.44-09.10.44	Rearguard of 8 British Army
10.10.44-01.01.45	Action in the Northern Apennines
02.01.45-08.04.45	Action on the River Senio
09.04.45-02.05.45	Battle for Bologna/Lombardy Plain

Medal Entitlement:

Polish: Cross for Valour, Cross of Monte Cassino No 23049

British: 1939-45 Star, Italy Star, Defence Medal, The War Medal 1939-45

APC
POLISH ENQUIRIES
RAF NORTHOLT

Yours faithfully

B Kroll

B KROLL (Mrs)
APC Polish Historical Disclosures

If you have any comments about the service you have received in response to your enquiry, please write to the following: Ms Beverly Hutchinson, Disclosures Manager, APC Support, MP 527, Kentigern House, 65 Brown Street, Glasgow G2 8EX

Family of Keith Wright (War diary extract)

Keith Wright's relative

Lance Sergeant John Henry Walstow

Part of a war dairy covering

April 1940 – 6th June 1940

Dunkirk evacuation.

1st June, 1940 Saturday

Wrote to Ivy. Meandered about all day. Very hot.

2nd June, 1940 Sunday

Church Parade in morning. Went walk in fields. Stood by all afternoon for departure to barracks. R. George went. Went walk round bathing pool at night. Naafi - eggs and mash!

3rd June, 1940 Monday

Went for paper at 7.30 a.m. Went for bathe in morning. Stood by in afternoon, Slept until 4.45 p.m. Went for tea to cafe. Went short walk at night with Wilf.

4th June, 1940 Tuesday

Reveille 5.00 a.m. Breakfast 5.15 a.m. Had buns and tea at little cafe. Dinner at 1.00. R.Q.M.S. etc. left us. Got letter from Ma. Wrote to Ivy, Ma and Harry. Slept in afternoon. Went walk at night.

5th June, 1940 Wednesday

Reveille 6.00 a.m. More left us. Parade at 10.00 a.m. Eventually went to Stanley Barracks and billeted in private house. Sunbathed with Wilf in afternoon and went to Naafi at night with Eddie Field and party after a walk round.

6th June, 1940 Thursday

Up at 6.00 a.m. Breakfast 6.30 a.m. Parade 7.30 a.m.. Put kit in 30 cwt. truck. Marched to station (Wool) travelled Ware~~mouth~~ham, Bournemouth, Poole, Southampton, Andover.

Family of Chris Nixon (Memoir extracts)

To Editor GGN

From Mrs Hilda Nixon

Subject "D" Day 1944 Contribution.

I joined the W.A.A.F. in 1941. After basic training I was posted to R.A.F. Northolt as a plotter in the operations room. Northolt was a fighter station, the pilots were all Polish, and very good fliers they were.

Volunteers were invited to learn Polish dancing and being fond of dancing I did. We performed at the camp concert, in London at the Polish Club; and eventually at The Cumberland Hotel at Marble Arch, where Ted Heath and his band were playing. He was a professional ballroom dancer and I had one dance with him. Quite an experience!

After two years my friend Jill and I were posted to R.A.F. Trimley near Felixstowe. This was a radar station which we found rather dull and quiet after busy Northolt. Early in 1944 we were posted to R.A.F. Uxbridge which controlled Eleven Group Fighter Command. When not too busy plotting we could gaze up into the Control and see Rex Harrison in his immaculate uniform but we never saw him actually doing anything - I suppose he was meant to be good for our moral!

After about two weeks things started to happen. First a visit by the King followed by General Eisenhour, General Montgomery and Air Marshal Tedder. This caused quite a buzz in the "ops" Room as you can guess.

Not long after this when going on night duty at midnight the operations table was a hive of activity; the south and south east coasts were full of plots of aircraft and shipping; the invasion had commenced and it was a busy and exciting night. As we came off duty that morning we were informed that we would not be allowed off station until news of the landings had been publicly announced.

Fortunately we did not have long to wait and after breakfast we were released. We sallied forth that morning at 10.30 down to Uxbridge High Street asking ourselves how could we celebrate ? Not very much at that hour, so resorting to custom we repaired to "The Fairy Bell" tea rooms and drank two cups of coffee instead of the usual one !

Eventually we were posted back to Trimley only to hear what fun the girls there had cycling to and from duty; the road having been completely lined with soldiers in tanks.

The end of the war was celebrated in the garden of our billet with one of the girls (no doubt with an American boyfriend) drinking neat gin in our mugs, Tasted horrible !

DRAFT

"CAPTURE BY CARRIER"
BY IVAN K. NIXON

EARLY ENCOUNTERS WITH DANGER

I'd had several "near misses" before being captured. The first was in early 1940 while still an Acting Unpaid Lance Corporal in the 12th Battalion of the Royal Sussex Regiment returning as one of a small group of newly-formed dispatch riders to our base camp near Abancourt; with those bell tents all in straight lines and without any camouflage. Having collected our motorbikes from Rouen nearby, we were bombed and straifed as we arrived back in broad daylight. Fortunately however everyone else had left, the battalion having been called to the front while we were away when the Germans broke through the Maginot (spelling?) Line.

The second time was on the 17th June 1940 when being evacuated from St Nazaire on the fall of France and having to abandon our trusty Norton 500 bikes we small band helped to give way to a Pioneer Battalion who then boarded the Lancastra, only to be bombed and sunk while still in the harbour with the tragic loss of many lives.

A third was common enough but considered useful experience at the time. It was again a direct bombing but this time while on a night exercise on Laffin Plain during my Officer Cadet Training Course at Aldershot.

THE CAPTURE

Having successfully transferred from the "P.B.I." to the Royal Engineers early in 1942 and become a 2nd Lieutenant i/c 3 Section in the 229 Army Field Company, it was while based at Thaxted, Essex during the autumn of 1942 that we received orders to prepare to go overseas and were duly issued with tropical kit. We boarded the old Cunard liner "Scythia" at Liverpool on the eleventh of November 1942 and then joined the main convoy assembling in the Firth of Clyde. We proceeded initially westwards out into the middle of the Atlantic when the purpose of our journey was first disclosed to us which was

- 1 -

Family of Sally Collins

WILLIAM EVELYN DOBSON-SMYTH
Squadron Leader (Spitfires) 1942-45
(Father of Sally Collins)

These are very sketchy stories that I remember being told by my father, William (Bill) Dobson-Smyth, of his experience as a Spitfire fighter pilot in WWII. Sadly all his logbooks were thrown out when my parents moved into a smaller house after we children had left home. He rarely talked about his wartime experiences and certainly never suggested that he was particularly brave or ever in any great danger!

He joined up at the age of 21 in 1942 suspending his studies as a medical student at Guys Hospital in London. His training in Yorkshire and Suffolk as a fighter pilot lasted about 5 weeks and then they were on their own. He missed the Battle of Britain which probably saved his life!

He trained Polish Spitfire fighter pilots possibly at Box Hill. Once when on a training exercise one of the trainee pilots came too close and clipped his wing. Both he and the trainee had to crash land.

He flew over the Atlantic escorting the Lancaster bombers to and from their targets.

He also spent some time in Egypt, mostly training pilots, but also enjoying bartering with the locals and exchanging cigarettes for watermelons!

He saw a lot of action towards the end of 1942 in Italy as the Germans retreated and shortly before Italy joined the Allies. He was mostly providing support to the bombing raids there and consequently felt guilty every time he subsequently visited Italy.

His Spitfire was shot down in Italy as the Germans were retreating and he was hidden by an Italian family who owned a vineyard. He thought he would go to the apparently abandoned German airfield and see if he could commandeer an airplane, only to find himself walking into an ongoing ambush by the Allies to capture the airfield from the few German soldiers left there. He was rugby tackled by some English soldiers and thrown into a ditch just before he compromised the whole mission.

He claimed to have been flying the first Allied aircraft to land in southern France, just as the German troops were leaving the airport, because he was running out of petrol.

Major Donald Collins, M.C.

South Wales Borderers

My father, Don Collins, joined the army on leaving school at the start of WWII. His regiment was the South Wales Borderers. He stayed in the army after the war, finally retiring from it in the late 1960s. He died in 1974.

I do not remember him talking much about his war experiences, we were just children when he died, and sadly there is no longer anyone around who can help with this.

As I remember it being told.......

He fought throughout the war, largely in France, Belgium and Holland, and he was wounded a number of times. Certainly, he had bullet wounds, but I think he also had shrapnel injuries. Somewhere we have binoculars with a bullet hole through them, representing a near miss.

In 1941 he had a serious motorcycle accident, a rope had been put at head height across a lane, maliciously, and he drove into it. It was suggested to his mother and father that they came quickly to visit him in hospital as it was thought he was unlikely to survive. He recovered, but he was left permanently deaf in one ear.

His wounds/injuries impacted on his later life. Although he was able to enjoy walking, sailing and the occasional game of golf, he was often unwell and required medical treatment. When he died quite suddenly at the age of 54, my mother was awarded a War Widow's Pension.

Enclosed in this folder:

A photo of him (date unknown)

His obituary from a local newspaper which provides quite a lot of interesting information about his army career.

Information about his Military Cross, awarded in 1944.

A photo of his medals.

Two telegrams and a letter relating to his Military Cross.

Telegrams and letters relating to his motorcycle accident

Letters from the relatives of men under his command who had died in battle. He had written to them to express his condolences, and these were their replies.

I hope you find the above interesting. I remember him as a devoted father, who died when I was much too young. I wish I had been able to have known him as an adult.

Family of Di Tatlock

(William Beardon 1944. Di's father)

The event in pictures

U.S.A.
2086490

WESSEX
INFANTRY

4
50
U.S. ARMY
XSV 422

50
U.S. ARMY
XSV 422

BATTLE OF BRITAIN
AUSTRALIA REMEMBERS
THE CHILDREN'S WAR
Daily Express

www.ingramcontent.com/pod-product-compliance
Ingram Content Group UK Ltd.
Pitfield, Milton Keynes, MK11 3LW, UK
UKHW062313290726
14090UKWH00018B/1052

9 781803 692227